Fred Astaire and Ginger Rogers: The Story of Hollywood's Most Famous Dancers

By Charles River Editors

Fred Astaire and Ginger Rogers in *The Barkleys of Broadway*

Introduction

Fred Astaire (1899-1987)

"No dancer can watch Fred Astaire and not know that we all should have been in another business." – Mikhail Baryshnikov

Virtually all famous actors are regaled by the public, but even still, Fred Astaire occupies a privileged position in American pop culture. The specific films in which Astaire acted may not be especially famous in their own right - most people likely cannot recall the title of *Top Hat* (1935), his most decorated film - but Astaire's dancing prowess invariably creates a lasting impact on viewers. Instead of tying his fame to a single film, Astaire's genius lay in constructing his star persona around a specific set of iconographic imagery that has become embedded within American culture. Across his films, the recurring iconic images of the top hat, cane, and coat tails, as well as the image of Astaire dancing with Ginger Rogers, all constitute a timeless symbol for elegance that continues to captivate viewers who are unfamiliar with the plots of his films. There have been other film musical actors who were proficient dancers, Gene Kelly chief among them, but none were able to perform with the seamless elegance of Astaire, and none have been remembered nearly as well.

Astaire's dancing numbers epitomized grace and gaiety, making it seem as though he was carefree, but this was hardly the case. While it is easy to imagine Astaire being raised in an aristocratic family, his working-class background was so blue collar that his family eventually relied on him and his sister as the primary breadwinners in the family. Rather than being born and raised with wealth in a large city, Astaire came from a working-class neighborhood in Omaha, Nebraska, a setting so antithetical to the world of dance that it quickly became clear that the family would need to relocate. If anything, Astaire's unglamorous origins further demonstrate that the magisterial dancing and the effortlessly elegant image accompanying it were products of Astaire's tireless work ethic and insistence on perfection.

Astaire's popularity can in large part be tied to the escapism that his films offered to impoverished Depression-era American audiences, and yet Astaire was a working man, albeit one who labored in the studios of Hollywood rather than the factories of America. Considering the quiet life that he led off the movie set, it can be difficult to disassociate Astaire from his films, and while he may have attempted to project the same image off the screen, the era and his personal background were extremely important. As someone who was born just before the start of the 20th century, Astaire's life sheds light on the developments that occurred in American entertainment, from the stage (where he first performed during his youth) to cinema (the site of his greatest triumphs) and finally to television (a medium Astaire entered at the end of his career.) Astaire's career tends to obscure his all-American success story, one in which hard work transformed a Nebraska boy from a working-class family into America's most prominent symbol of grace.

This book profiles the life and career of Astaire with a bibliography and pictures of important people, places, and events. You will learn about Fred Astaire like you never have before.

Ginger Rogers (1911-1995)

"I adored Fred. We were good friends. Our only problem is that we never aspired to be any kind of a team. We didn't want to be Abbott and Costello. We thought of ourselves as individuals. We didn't intend to be another Frick and Frack. But it happened anyway, didn't it? And I'll be forever grateful it did." – Ginger Rogers

There is no denying that the career of Ginger Rogers cannot be entirely divorced from that of Fred Astaire. The unlikely pairing - Rogers was a statuesque blonde while Astaire fell well short of the masculine ideal expected of male movie stars - only made their screen romance more dreamlike, even as the physical contrasts between them melted away during their protracted dance numbers. Not only were Astaire and Rogers the preeminent box office attraction of the time period, but they remain the most recognizable faces of the musical genre as a whole. It is telling that, as Edward Gallafent notes, the duo are identified simply as Fred and Ginger, with no need to even provide their last names. Moreover, not only are films such as Top Hat (1935) and Shall We Dance (1937) cornerstones of the musical, but one of the great achievements of the Fred and Ginger team is that they never fell out of public favor. Indeed, the completeness of the Fred and Ginger pairing was punctuated by the fact that there was no bitter breakup between them, making it so that audiences are left only with the seamless screen romances between them.

Considering the immense success of their films together, it is entirely understandable that Astaire and Rogers are joined at the hip in the eyes of the public. However, an appreciation for the Fred and Ginger musicals is only enhanced by knowledge of the personal backgrounds of the two stars. After all, the fact remains that Astaire and Rogers came from vastly different cultural backgrounds, and at the time that they met, their careers had unfolded in dissimilar ways. Astaire was a national celebrity for his skills as a stage performer (mainly with his sister Adele), while Rogers was raised in a more archetypal Midwestern setting and her professional success was reached entirely through cinema. While Astaire made a name for himself through his dancing, Rogers was more recognized for her singing talents. Clearly, it is still possible to discern fundamental differences between their professional talents, contrasts that would become more distinguishable once they ceased making films together.

Along with pictures of important people, places, and events, you will learn about Ginger Rogers like you never have before.

Chapter 1: Fred's Early Years

"Old is like everything else. To make a success of it, you've got to start young." – Fred Astaire

Frederick Austerlitz II was born on May 10, 1899, with a name that could not seem more different than the one he would come to be known by. In fact, the difference between Fred's real last name and the name he was given in Hollywood is significant, because Astaire intentionally evoked a French etymology, whereas his birth name reflected Prussian heritage. The young boy's name was an homage to his father, Frederic "Fritz" Austerlitz (the only difference being that his father had no "k" at the end of his first name). Meanwhile, Astaire's mother was Johanna "Ann" Geilus. Fred had an older sister, Adele, who was two-and-a-half years his senior.

Fred's parents came from very different backgrounds. His father, Fritz, was born in Austria and was raised in a traditional Prussian family. The pedigree of his family is still not entirely clear, but it is believed that his family was Jewish before converting to Catholicism, and Fritz was raised Catholic. Born in 1868, it was not until he was an adult that he moved to the United States. In fact, throughout his adolescence Fritz had no clear aspirations of relocating across the Atlantic; it was only after he was punished by the Austro-Hungarian Army in 1892 that he decided to move (Epstein). The circumstances surrounding his punishment are possibly apocryphal, as they were retold frequently over the years, but it was said that Fritz was an officer in the Austro-Hungarian Army alongside his two brothers, Otto and Ernst. Since Ernst was his superior, Fritz was required to salute his elder brother, and when he failed to do so, his brother (who was very bureaucratic in nature) orchestrated his imprisonment (Levinson). While staying in prison, Fritz realized that he did not intend to spend his adult life in the army, so he made the decision to immigrate to the United States (Epstein).

When Fritz arrived at Ellis Island in 1892, he had aspirations of achieving great wealth, but naturally there weren't many lucrative employment opportunities for newly arriving immigrants, and he was relegated to pursuing menial jobs. After a short while, he and a small group of Austrian friends moved to Omaha, where they intended to start a business publishing studio photographs. Even though Fritz was not skilled in operating a camera, his jovial disposition was well-suited for interacting with the public, making him a good fit for the position of company salesman. Unfortunately for Fritz and his colleagues, the economic Panic of '93 ruined the company, which went bankrupt shortly after they set it up in Omaha. (Levinson). In the bad economy, opportunities were scarce, and Fritz eventually accepted a job working as a salesman in a brewery.

In contrast with Fritz, Fred's mother, Johanna, came from a more subdued background. While Fritz was gregarious and a natural salesman, Johanna was shy and worked as a schoolteacher. The two met shortly after Fritz's arrival in Omaha, and their relationship was expedited when Johanna got pregnant. It was socially frowned-upon to raise a family prior to getting married, and it is quite possible that Fritz and Johanna would have never gotten married if not for the unplanned pregnancy.

Even though no one could deny Fritz's charm, his in-laws had legitimate reasons to worry about their daughter marrying Fritz. Johanna was just 17 years old when she got pregnant, an especially young age to give birth to a child, and she was eight years younger than Fritz as well. Moreover, Fritz had done nothing to prove that he could sustain employment, and while the failure of the photography studio was not his fault, the fact remained that he had yet to demonstrate that he could provide for Johanna and their child. Nevertheless, Fritz and Johanna got married ahead of the baby's birth, only to lose the baby anyway. (Epstein). It would not be until two years later that Johanna would give birth to their first child, Adele, and Fred followed in 1899.

Over the course of Fred Astaire's life, he would benefit from good fortune on many occasions, which was ironic considering that clearly was not the case for his father. Fritz would continue to be a failed businessman, despite having ambition and a strong work ethic, and he and Johanna settled into a lower-middle class environment in Omaha, with Fritz continuing to work at the brewery while Johanna tended to the children. Still, for all of the differences between Fred's parents, they were each highly ambitious, with Johanna yearning to escape Omaha and Fritz wanting his children to succeed.

Like many young boys, Fred was fascinated by trains and enjoyed the many trains that passed through the Omaha landscape, but his upbringing was hardly a normal one, because it quickly became evident that Fred and his sister exhibited precocious talent as singers and dancers. When Fred was two years of age, Adele was enrolled in the Chambers Dancing Academy in Omaha, and after she demonstrated her innate talents as a dancer, Fred began taking classes himself. Since Adele began dancing training before her brother, it's evident that Fred's career owes a great debt to his sister, since he followed in her lead throughout his childhood. Not only did Adele possess great physical talent, but it was immediately clear from a young age that she was a great beauty (Epstein). Her dazzling appearance stands in stark contrast to Fred's unremarkable appearance as an adult, but it was Fred who was the outlier; both of Fred's parents were very attractive, and Adele inherited her mother's soft eyes and dark hair.

Fred and Adele performing vaudeville circa 1906

The siblings performed together even as young children, but their success rose as Fritz's professional fortunes diminished. By 1902, he had worked for the Omaha Brewers Association since arriving in the city nine years earlier, but that year the company was bought out by Storz Brewery. Fritz was not forced to relinquish his job altogether, but he had to take a pay cut. Around this time, he also began drinking heavily and (allegedly) having affairs, though Fred would later adamantly claim that his family environment as a young child was peaceful (Levinson). Still, Fritz's lack of success meant that the Astaires were in no way beholden to the Omaha region; Johanna's parents lived there, but she had long yearned to move away herself. If anything, it seemed the talents of their children might be the way in which the entire family could get out.

Thus, even though Fritz and Johanna did not possess any talents that would facilitate their relocation to another city, they could rationalize the family's departure due to the fact their children, particularly Adele, were too talented to receive sufficient dancing instruction in the Midwest. Moreover, due to her husband's behavior, Adele was not bothered by the possibility of living apart from her husband, so long as he provided for the family as best he could. As a result, Fred's parents began looking into the possibilities of moving even before Fred entered the first grade.

Ultimately, it was decided that Fred, Adele, and Johanna would relocate to New York City, and they moved there in 1905. Although Fred and his sister would eventually achieve great fame, the move was entirely motivated by naiveté; Johanna improbably believed that her daughter (and possibly her son, if lucky) could quickly gain training as top-flight dancers and begin supporting the family. While they received their training, Fritz was to send money and subsidize their schooling at the dance school. What Fred did not realize at the time (only to eventually disclose in his autobiography) was that he and his sister had not even gained acceptance at the dancing institution before the move:

> "As I learned years later, this trip was really a stab in the dark. We were going to New York without so much as a letter of introduction to somebody's aunt. My mother had never been there, and she knew no one, theatrical or otherwise. She had not even written ahead to enroll us in a dancing school. So none of the Astaires could have known what was in store for them." (Astaire 14)

Astaire's description suggests a bit of Midwestern innocence, as though no one in his family could have known what was in store for them in the big city. However, this is perhaps unfair, because Fritz had lived in New York City after arriving to Ellis Island. While his stay had been more than a decade earlier, it is still surprising that he had not warned Johanna and his children of the improbability of achieving any success in such an immense, competitive environment. The fact Fritz supported the move reflects his idealism, the same idealism that led him to expect to earn great riches after emigrating from Europe to America years earlier.

Astaire would later note in his autobiography that upon getting off the train, he looked around and remarked to his sister, "This is a big city." She tartly replied, "This is only the depot." Of course, New York was the big city at the time, and when Fred, his mother, and his sister arrived there in 1905, they stayed at the Herald Square Hotel. As with many hotels of the time period, the hotel acted as a boarding residence of sorts, with guests remaining for extended visits (Levinson).

After securing residence, Johanna enrolled her children in dancing school. Even though they had not yet been admitted, she, Fritz, and her children's dancing instructor at Omaha identified the Claude Alvienne Dance School, located at Grand Opera House Building, as a suitable institution. Shortly after arriving in New York City, the Astaires began their dancing instruction at the dance school, attending classes during the day, and after returning to their residence at the hotel, Johanna taught them more traditionally academic subjects, a task for which she was well-suited given her experience working as a school teacher in Omaha. Astaire later remembered, "I simply did not get the idea that dancing was for me. However, I took it as a matter of course. It seemed natural enough to go with Adele and do what she did."

The Claude Alvienne Dance School was not an educational institution in the traditional sense, as students were not expected attend for years on end. Rather, it served a vocational purpose, offering intense instruction with the expectation that students would quickly gain the skills needed to succeed in the dancing profession. That children were placed in such an explicitly vocational setting may seem tantamount to child abuse, but Fred would later look back on his time at the dance school with fondness, claiming that the exercises were not disagreeable and that the instructors were nurturing and gentle (Astaire). Noting that the instructor would never scold students but would tell them if they did something wrong by hitting a chair with a stick, Astaire wrote, "I still had no urge to dance, but I loved that stick."

Shortly after enrolling in the school, the benevolent Claude Alvienne (founder of the school) would prove instrumental in securing roles for Fred and his sister. Before they performed professionally, however, Alvienne advised the Astaires that in order to achieve success they would need to change their name. "Austerlitz" was difficult to pronounce and sounded too foreign, while "Astaire" was far more marketable. Around the same time, Johanna also changed her own name by shortening it to "Anna" (Epstein). By this time, the siblings were perfecting dancing acts together, some of which had them playing bride and groom, and as their vaudeville picture from 1906 indicates, Fred and Adele appeared very comfortable before the camera. There is no trace of self-consciousness, and any trace of the children's Omaha background seemed to have already vanished. Not only does Fred don a stylish outfit that predates the top-hats that he would later make his signature, but Adele appears in an ornate, florid outfit that connotes an upper-class upbringing. From an early age, Fred and Adele had the ability to give off a sense of elegance and class that was not traced to their family heritage.

Alvienne was able to use his connections in order to schedule bookings for Fred and Adele to perform, but the Astaire children were also assisted by their father. Despite spending the majority of his time in Omaha, Fritz made frequent trips to New York City, and when he could be there, he parlayed his salesman charm to good effect, establishing strong connections with theater managers and other influential figures within the industry. Through the assistance of Fritz and Claude Alvienne, Fred and Adele remained busy and earned a moderate income for the family performing all throughout the East Coast (Levinson). There is some disagreement over the site of their first professional performance, but it's believed to have been either in Newport, Rhode Island or Keyport, New Jersey (Levinson). Astaire later joked, "The Keyport newspaper proclaimed, 'The Astaires are the greatest child act in vaudeville.' I think if two words had been added, 'in Keyport', this might have been more accurate."

In their first years performing together, the Astaires performed most often in New Jersey and Pennsylvania. In New Jersey, they made stops in Atlantic City, Perth Amboy, Passaic, Paterson, Newark, and Union Hill; Pennsylvania trips included Philadelphia, Pottsdown, and Lancaster. Traveling along the East Coast gave the Astaire children valuable experience, but their first major break came when they were signed to a high-profile contract to perform along the Orpheum Circuit, a vaudeville circuit that would eventually become subsumed by the RKO film studio. Performing along the Orpheum Circuit led to Fred and Adele traveling to more distant locales, including Pennsylvania, Iowa, Colorado, Washington, D.C., California, Utah, Nebraska,

Minnesota, and Wisconsin (Levinson). It is important to remember that the vaudeville circuit effectively served as the predecessor to cinema; years later, films would be exhibited throughout the country, but during the early years of the motion picture medium, the American public enjoyed vaudeville and other popular forms of entertainment (baseball being a notable example) instead.

As Fred and Adele grew older, Adele's physical growth threatened the success of their act. As she neared her teenage years, it became increasingly unconvincing for both siblings to play young children. Due to her stunning beauty, it would not necessarily have been difficult for Adele to secure appearances on the vaudeville circuit, but the children's act that she and Fred had perfected over the previous several years became untenable. Making matters worse, as they became better-known throughout the Orpheum Circuit, the Astaire siblings faced the scrutiny of the Gerry Agency, and they were forced to lie about their ages in order to comply with child labor laws. It was illegal for children to work to the extent that Fred and Adele were, and while Fred would later give no indication that he was displeased with the heavy performance schedule, it was clear that it would be impossible to continue the routine as it had operated.

One aspect of Fred and Adele's success that is easily overlooked is the role played by their mother. Johanna possessed a shrewd business sense and understood that it would pay dividends over time for her children to take a hiatus from acting (Levinson). Not only would this appease the Gerry Agency, but Fred and Adele could resume their careers after Fred caught up with his sister physically. Moreover, they could use their "sabbatical" to good effect by rehearsing new material and transforming their act from one involving little children to one featuring more age-appropriate material.

During their two-year break from performing, which took place in 1909 and 1910, Fred and Adele relocated with their mother to Weehawken, New Jersey, a working-class neighborhood. At this time, Fritz remained in Omaha, and the marriage between him and Johanna suffered from the effects of their estrangement. Johanna learned that Fritz lived with another woman in their Omaha house, and Fritz continued to drink heavily — Fred would indeed grow up to be an entirely different person from his father. Meanwhile, in New Jersey, Fred enrolled in the 5th grade, his first exposure to formal education. In 1911, the teenagers enrolled in the Ned Wayburn's school in New York City, where the Astaires resumed their training in the dramatic arts. Even though they had achieved great success for their age, they were still relatively untrained in areas such as dance, ballet, and singing, but at the Ned Wayburn's school, they received valuable instruction in these areas. In yet another shrewd move, Johanna also paid Wayburn $1,000 to devise a new routine for her children, an investment that would pay dividends over the next several years.

Immediately after returning to performing, Fred and Adele experienced adversity and negative reviews. Their return to the stage occurred in February of 1912, where they performed at the

Proctor's Fifth Avenue Vaudeville Theatre, but they were poorly received and the engagement was not sustainable. The following year proved to be no better, as Fred began suffering from worrying bouts of anxiety, a surprising problem in light of the ultra-confident aura he would project in his later film roles. However, Astaire would in fact suffer from anxiety during his entire career, a tendency that would actually prove productive because it led to a tireless perfectionism. In contrast, Adele was far less driven than her brother and felt less of a need to rehearse and perfect the routines and rapport between the two siblings. The two were also polar opposites; Fred was socially conservative and became an Episcopalian in 1912 (remaining devoutly religious for the rest of his life), while Adele was a free spirit who was unafraid to cuss or flaunt her sexuality (Levinson).

Unsurprisingly, the difference in their personalities and approaches led to a shift in the talent dynamic between the Fred and his sister. For the first decade or so of their career, Adele was deemed by far the more talented of the two, but over time there was a gradual shift that led to Fred being considered by far the more adept. Indeed, Epstein notes, "Without Adele as his dancing partner at the beginning of his career, Fred Astaire might have ended up as a suburban husband, selling swank high-line cars (for which he had a lifelong taste). In their early years as a dance team, Adele supplied the main excitement. But the commitment to perfection was not in her in a way that it was in her brother." (10). While Adele may well have been more gifted than her brother and assisted in giving her brother his first exposure to the world of professional entertainment, Fred's unmatched work ethic separated him from her and played an instrumental role in his later success. Actress and dancer Nanette Fabray later said about Fred, "He was a dictator who made me work harder and longer than anyone."

After weathering the adversity that initially greeted their return to performing, the Astaires achieved more success than ever before in 1914. Around that time, they enlisted the services of Aurelia Coccia, who taught Fred how to tap dance. Over the past year, it had become clear that Fred needed a new skill in order to remain successful, and tap dancing offered a niche that separated him from others in the industry. They began securing more bookings, appearing first throughout New England and then expanding their demographic. Fred and Adele earned $350 per week, more than double what they had made years earlier on the Orpheum circuit. Over time their price continued to escalate, and in 1917 they made their debut on Broadway with the show *Over the Top*. Their price rose, and they soon began commanding $550 per week.

In 1918, the siblings appeared in the Broadway show *Apple Blossoms*, which endured a long run that would last until 1920. During this period, the Astaires were also hired by the Brothers Shubert to appear in *The Passing Show of 1918*, and critic Heywood Broun wrote of their performance, "In an evening in which there was an abundance of good dancing, Fred Astaire stood out ... He and his partner, Adele Astaire, made the show pause early in the evening with a beautiful loose-limbed dance." That performance also brought them into contact with performers such as Al Jolson, Fanny Brice, and Charlie Ruggles (Epstein). Fred and his sister had not only rebounded from the disappointment of 1912 and 1913 but soared to greater heights than they had achieved during their early years performing together. By 1920, the Astaires found themselves in the upper strata of society, mingling with the wealthy elite of New York and Philadelphia, and as they began earning more money, they began to adopt a more liberal (though not reckless) attitude with their money, staying in high-end hotels and spending more freely. Performing in Atlantic City, Fred took an interest in craps and poker, and he began to make room for leisure in his crowded routine (Levinson). In addition, they began performing abroad in London, where they were exposed to British culture, which would have a profound influence on Fred and his sister.

Chapter 2: Ginger's Early Years

"I don't know which I like best. I love the applause on the stage. But pictures are so fascinating - you reach many millions through them. And you make more money too." – Ginger Rogers

Ginger Rogers was born on July 16, 1911 in Independence, Missouri, and like many Hollywood stars of her era, the name given to her at birth was far different from the one she would later be remembered by. The baby girl was born Virginia Katherine McMath to parents William Eddins McMath and Lela Emogene Owens, and she would later muse, "My mother told me I was dancing before I was born. She could feel my toes tapping wildly inside her for months."

Virginia was an only child, due mostly to the fact that her parents separated almost immediately after she was born. William worked as an electrical engineer, and in an age in which career women were relatively scarce, Lela worked continuously throughout Ginger's childhood, first as a secretary, then as a script writer, and finally as a theater critic (Faris).

Ginger as a child

After Lela and Williams were divorced, a fierce custody battle ensued concerning Ginger. Ultimately, Lela was given the right to raise her daughter, with William denied any visitation rights. As a result, on two occasions William attempted to forcefully remove his daughter from Lela's possession, and while he was able to extricate Ginger from Lela's possession, she was ultimately returned to her mother.

When the divorce was finalized and Lela was forced to find employment, she left for Hollywood to work as a scriptwriter. She would later leave for New York City to work as a scriptwriter (living away from her daughter for a full two years), and between her time in California and New York, she would write for luminaries such as Theda Bara, Gladys Brockwell, and Baby Marie Osborne (Faris). Even if she was not an actress in her own right, Lela's writing abilities reflected an instinct for show business and the type of material that would captivate an audience.

The close bond between Ginger Rogers and her mother is well-documented, which is somewhat surprising considering she was raised by her maternal grandparents more than Lela during her early childhood. When Lela left for Hollywood and New York City, Ginger was sent from Independence to Kansas City, Missouri, where she stayed with Walter and Saphrona Owens. The family was especially religious, and she was raised a Christian Scientist. Despite having a firm bond with her mother, living with her grandparents was not unwelcome for Ginger, and she would remain close to them after beginning her Hollywood career, going so far as to purchase a home for them in Hollywood. She never harbored any resentment for her humble origins, and even after becoming an internationally renowned professional actress, the urban nature of Hollywood and show business would never entirely obscure her preference for rural life. In fact, she would later complain, "Hollywood is like an empty wastebasket."

Hollywood tended to change the names for their biggest stars, but that's not how Virginia McMath became Ginger Rogers. Instead, the nickname Ginger came about during his youth. In a sense, this should come as no surprise; it was common for Hollywood to instruct its starlets to change their name, but she was not actually a redhead so it would have been strange to instruct her to adopt "Ginger" as a name. As a child, one her younger cousins, Helen, had difficulty pronouncing "Virginia" and instead used to pronounce it like Ginger. Thus, instead of referring to her hair color, the name Ginger came about simply because it was easier for her cousin to pronounce. Ginger Rogers would be known as Ginger McMath for several years during her youth.

Ginger McMath would get a new last name after Lela returned from scriptwriting and remarried, this time to John Logan Rogers, an ex-Marine. The couple were married in Liberty, Missouri, but they departed soon after the wedding and relocated to Fort Worth, Texas, where John Logan Rogers was to begin a job with an insurance company in Texas. When Lela remarried, Ginger took the name of her mother's new husband, despite the fact that he never legally adopted her. Regardless, moving to Fort Worth brought a sense of stability to the young girl's upbringing, as Fort Worth would be the city where she received her education.

Given the trials and tribulations associated with the first decade of her life, one might expect that Rogers would grow up as an unhappy or anxiety-ridden child, but this was hardly the case. Even though her biological father attempted to forcefully gain possession of her, Ginger lost contact with him entirely and she was instead raised by loving figures throughout her childhood, whether with her grandparents in Kansas City or her mother in Fort Worth. Still, there is no denying that from an early age, Rogers was faced with considerable adversity, particularly in light of the fact that she was raised in an era in which divorce was rare. That Rogers was able to face challenging circumstances with a positive outlook reflects the optimism that would constitute a cornerstone of her identity as a major Hollywood star.

During the first decade and a half of her upbringing, there was no way of predicting that Ginger would eventually become an actress, despite her mother's success as a scriptwriter. As a young girl, she instead dreamed of one day working as a schoolteacher (Faris). She did star in her school plays, but this was hardly unusual, and Ginger had a diverse array of interests, from singing to acting to athletics. The first hint that Ginger might be destined for a career in show business occurred in November of 1925, when she was honored as the Texas State Charleston Champion, a success that gave her the opportunity to embark on a four year vaudeville tour throughout the country. This allowed Ginger to perform around the country in places like

Boston, Pittsburgh, St. Louis, Phoenix, Los Angeles, Atlanta, and New York City (Faris). She and her mother made a natural team; Ginger performed the material, while Lela wrote all of the scripts and designed Ginger's costumes (Faris). Despite enrolling in Central High School in Fort Worth, Ginger did not graduate, as her success on the vaudeville tour effectively declared that acting would be her profession.

When Rogers performed on the vaudeville circuit, she demonstrated a formidable ability to engage with her audience. The skill set needed for vaudeville comedy was diverse; not only was Rogers a strong dancer, but she was a great singer and was a natural when it came to comedic delivery. It is worth noting that Ginger and former dance partner Fred Astaire were both performing on stage during this time period (though to be fair, Astaire was far more decorated than Rogers during the 1920s), but all of Astaire's success was tied to his ability to dance (he had no real talent as a singer), whereas Rogers possessed many abilities, all of which would be put to great use during her film career in Hollywood.

From 1925-1929, Ginger's vaudeville career was prolific, ensuring that she had consistent employment. Another major development that occurred during these years was her first marriage. In 1927, at just 17 years of age, she married Jack Culpepper, a performer who worked as a singer, dancer, and comedian, the same talents that Ginger possessed. It's interesting to note that she did not change her name, perhaps due to being leery of committing herself in this manner after witnessing her mother's difficult first marriage. Nevertheless, given their similar talents, it was only natural for Ginger and Culpepper to form a vaudeville team, and they performed under the title "Ginger and Pepper."

Even by the standards of the time period, 17 was a particularly young age to marry, but there were several reasons to believe that the relationship would last even aside from their similar professional interests. Ginger had known Culpepper for years, because he had previously been romantically involved with her cousin. However, the marriage was fraught with conflict from the start, and it would prove to be just the first of many tumultuous marriages for Ginger. She and Culpepper were separated within months of marrying, ending their professional partnership as well, although it would not be until 1931 that they formally divorced.

Ginger in 1932, before she went blonde.

Separating from Culpepper was not only a necessary decision on a personal level but would also pay dividends professionally as well. Shortly after ending her relationship with her husband, Ginger resumed touring the vaudeville circuit with her mother, and while in New York City, she began securing jobs singing for radio. As with most actresses of the time period, Ginger's career thus owes a great debt to the developments that were made in technology and mass culture. In an earlier era, it's an open question whether she would have ever been able to reach the mass audience she acquired through radio. By contrast, the popularity she enjoyed as a result of her radio career would flow seamlessly into success in the theatre and then ultimately in the motion picture industry. On a related note, the achievements in recorded sound that were reached via radio facilitated the monumental development of synchronized sound that first occurred in film with *The Jazz Singer* in 1928. It would not be incorrect to state that Rogers was introduced to audiences through her voice rather than her body, a dynamic that is surprising considering her later dancing feats but indicative of the changes in mass media that were made during the last half of the 1920s.

Before Rogers became a film actress, she first starred in the theatre, working concurrently in radio and theatre while living in New York City with her mother. Her first appearance on

Broadway was in *Top Speed*, which opened on Christmas Day in 1929 and would later be adapted as a film the following year. The show lasted less than five months and Ginger was not featured in the headlining role, but the high-profile venue ensured that Ginger acquired substantial publicity and suggested that she could have a profitable career in Hollywood. Building on *Top Speed*, she was then cast in the starring role in *Girl Crazy*. The play (a musical) featured Rogers in the role of Molly Gray, a postmistress for a small Arizona ranching town. As one would expect, the plot merely fills the gaps left by the songs, which were written by George and Ira Gershwin. Rogers sang "Could You Use Me" and "Embraceable You," and the production is also remembered for the songs performed by Ethel Merman, notably "I Got Rhythm" and "Boy! What Has Love Done to Me!" *Girl Crazy* was a major production, and in an unlikely turn of events, it was on the set of the play that Rogers would first meet Fred Astaire, who had been hired as a consultant for the dance routines. The play was a far greater success than *Top Speed*, lasting from October 14, 1930 through June 6, 1931, a run that included 271 performances in total.

Shortly after she first began receiving recognition for her work in radio and theatre, Ginger received her first acting jobs in cinema. During the late 1920s and early 1930s, the film industry had not yet completed its wide-scale migration from New York City to California, so it was still possible for Rogers to work in theatre and film at the same time. In 1929, she was discovered by Paramount and signed to a seven-year contract. That same year, she appeared in three small-scale non-feature films for Paramount: *A Day of a Man of Affairs* (1929), *A Night in a Dormitory* (1930), and *Campus Sweethearts* (1930). In 1930, she appeared in her first feature film, *Young Man of Manhattan* (1930), which starred Claudette Colbert and Norman Foster as a married couple that experience discord when Foster's character realizes that his wife earns more money than he does. Rogers appears as Puff Randolph (a flapper) and delivers the most memorable line in an otherwise unmemorable film: "Puff me, cigarette boy." Envisioning Rogers as a flapper may seem unlikely in light of the wholesome image she projected both in her films with Fred Astaire and afterward, but she liked performing various roles, which also showed off her versatility as an actress and made it easier to avoid pigeonholing herself as a B-movie character actress. According to Jocelyn Faris, this flexibility as an actress was a strategy designed by Lela that would pay dividends throughout Rogers's career: "Ginger's longevity as a star was due to Lela's continually expanding her daughter's movie roles and persona instead of allowing her daughter to be stereotyped into one type of role (3)." This description may seem ironic (and incongruous) in light of the fact that Ginger would be forever linked with Fred Astaire in the eyes of the public, but her early performances did demonstrate a strong degree of versatility, shifting from innocent young women to flappers.

Late 1930 and early 1931 was an extraordinarily busy period for Rogers, who acted in films for Paramount during the day and appeared in *Girl Crazy* at night. By July of 1931, she had appeared in five feature films for Paramount, which were shot at Astoria Studios in Queens. When *Girl Crazy* ended its run in July, Ginger realized that it was in her best interest to make a decision between becoming a stage actress and a film star. On the surface, there was good reason for her to consider remaining in New York, especially since she had just starred in one of the most high-profile productions in recent years. However, despite headlining the show, Rogers had been compensated just $1,000 per week for *Girl Crazy*, a wage that was certainly robust for Depression-era America but significantly less than the salary commanded by a prominent movie actress.

Ginger in *Girl Crazy*

If she intended to pursue cinema, it was untenable to remain in New York City; Paramount was an outlier by continuing to produce films in New York City, and most other studios had long migrated cross-country to California. The advantages in California included preferable weather, especially with warmer temperatures that made it far easier to shoot during winter. The comparably undeveloped landscape also allowed studios to build elaborate set designs that were impossible to create in the crowded New York City streets. Realizing that she preferred cinema to theatre and that Hollywood would inevitably be the site for her professional advancement, she requested that her contract with Paramount be terminated. At her behest, the studio acquiesced, and Rogers and her mother made the move to Hollywood during the summer of 1931.

Chapter 3: Getting a Start in Hollywood

"He is a truly complex fellow, not unlike the Michelangelos and da Vincis of the Renaissance period. He's a supreme artist but he is constantly filled with doubts and self-anger about his work--and that is what makes him so good. He is a perfectionist who is never sure he is attaining perfection." - Rouben Mamoulian

One of the great formative experiences of Astaire's entire career was his first trip to London, which not only exposed him to a foreign culture for the first time but one that would form the foundation for his star persona. Epstein elaborates, "On his first trip to England, Fred Astaire turned from a young man who was well-groomed and carefully dressed into someone close to what used to be called a fashion plate. He became mid-Atlantic in his taste in clothes; his speech, with its splendidly clear diction, seemed a touch mid-Atlantic, too. He found himself admiring the clothes of the British aristocracy." (36)

Of course, working as a performer meant that spending money on clothes was not only a personal hobby but also a business investment. Through effecting a well-heeled fashion style, Astaire only strengthened his stage persona, and it was during this period that the Fred Astaire identity was formulated. He was not born into wealth or knowledge of fashion but quickly learned how to present himself with an air of sophistication that made it seem as though he had been born into royalty.

Adele in 1919

Fred in 1920

By 1920, Fred and Adele commanded $750 per week, and as they began earning greater sums of money, they were introduced to prominent cultural figures. The Astaires counted Tallulah Bankhead, Gertrude Lawrence, and Noel Coward among their friends, and they moved into the Carlton Hotel in Manhattan. The 1920s were a period of great financial and cultural triumph for Fred and Adele, and they proved that it was possible to progress from childhood success to adult triumph. In 1924, they appeared in George and Ira Gershwin's *Lady Be Good* (1924), which was performed on Broadway, and three years later, they would appear in another Gershwin production, *Funny Face*, that also included runs on Broadway and in London. By this time, it was clear that even though Adele was an adept dancer in her own right, Fred possessed the generational talent, and his work ethic ensured his talent continued growing. One of the benefits of residing in New York City was that the city not only provided a diverse array of performing venues but also allowed Astaire to learn from the artistic customs of different cultures. He frequently visited Harlem, learning from and appropriating the tap dancing talents of popular performers there during the late 1920s (Levinson).

The Astaires remained in high demand throughout the decade, but the contrasting personalities of the two siblings eventually created an impasse. Where Fred was ambitious and dynamic, Adele was more passive and ultimately disinterested in furthering her career. After all, by the start of the 1930s, Fred was widely considered the top dancer in the world, a designation that Adele could not hope to equal (Mueller). As American writer Robert Benchley put it in 1930, "I don't think that I will plunge the nation into war by stating that Fred is the greatest tap-dancer in the world." Despite the fact that they had risen to fame through the success of their teamwork, Astaire was driven in a way that his sister was not, and their final show together occurred in

1931. Titled *The Band Wagon*, the show first ran in June of 1931 and lasted for 261 performances.

Fred and Adele performing in 1921

After *The Band Wagon*, Adele retired and married Lord Charles Arthur Francis Cavendish, the Son of the Duke of Devonshire. The marriage was a tumultuous one, fraught with conflicts resulting from Cavendish's addiction to alcohol. He would eventually pass away in 1944 and remained married to Adele through the end of his life. At the time of Adele's courtship to Lord Charles, Fred began taking an interest in women for the first time. Naturally much shier than his sister, he was bashful around women and had difficulty talking with them. However, beginning in 1931, Astaire began a relationship with Phyllis Potter, a wealthy Boston socialite who had not even heard of him at the time they met (Epstein). The relationship was frowned upon by Adele and Astaire's mother, largely due to the fact that Phyllis had already been married to Eliphalet Nott Potter III, but after a brief courtship, they were married in 1933, beginning a long and healthy marriage. Astaire would later frame his married life with Phyllis in idyllic terms: "Phyllis was an extraordinary girl. We were always together other than in my working hours. She seldom came to the studios…At the completion of a film, we would travel abroad or go on shooting and fishing trips here. I usually managed three months off between pictures. Weekends during productions were spent at our Blue Valley Ranch, which she loved so much. We established that in 1950." (6)

Astaire's marriage with Phyllis highlights that even as his career became increasingly more glamorous throughout the 1930s, his personal life remained quiet. Still, while his personal life settled down during the early 1930s, the retirement of his sister left him looking for a new female partner with whom to perform. From 1931-1933, he danced alongside Claire Luce, a talented dancer, but initially, Fred's shyness made their rapport awkward. He eventually grew accustomed to working with her, thanks in part to prodding from Luce, who reminded him he could add more romantic undertones to the performances by saying, "Come on, Fred, I'm not your sister, you know." In 1932, they starred together in *The Gay Divorce*, a production that is remembered for featuring Cole Porter's hit song "Night and Day." The play would be Astaire's final Broadway show, and also enjoyed a run in London. Two years later, after Fred had begun acting in Hollywood, it would later be adapted for the cinema by RKO with Fred reprising his role.

Astaire and Luce in *Gay Divorce* on Broadway in 1932

By 1933, Astaire had just gained a spouse but lost his longtime professional partner in Adele. Adele would later be asked why she didn't perform with her brother in Hollywood, and she replied, "If people would only realize when they ask me why I don't do a picture with him - they ask me that all the time, and were quite keen on it while I was in Hollywood - if they'd only realize that he's gone 'way ahead of me. Why I couldn't begin to keep up with him. I couldn't even reach the steps he throws away."

Even though he and Luce were successful together, his partnership with Luce would prove to be short-lived. Instead of returning to Broadway, Astaire looked to Hollywood for his next career venture. In fact, his foray into cinema was not his first attempt to do so. Several years earlier, he and Adele had explored the possibility of acting on screen, but to no avail. Still, his past failure did not prevent RKO from signing him to a contract, and 1933 is credited as the year that he first broke into the motion picture industry. The man who signed Astaire, David Selznick, wrote at the time, "I am uncertain about the man, but I feel, in spite of his enormous ears and bad chin line, that his charm is so tremendous that it comes through even on this wretched test."

The major difference between Astaire's first attempt to break into Hollywood and his successful entry in 1933 was not that he had grown substantially as a dancer. Rather, the major difference was that by 1933, synchronized sound had come into existence, leading to the rise of the Musical as one of the preeminent genres in Hollywood. Astaire's dancing prowess would still have been a visual attraction during the silent era, but his physicality was significantly more arresting when accompanied by singing and a musical score. In this regard, it is not unreasonable to attribute Astaire's rise to fame in large part to the developments that occurred to the cinematic medium between the late 1920s and early 1930s.

Fred was by no means old when he entered Hollywood, but it is nevertheless important to note that he was no longer a young adult either. The fact that he had so long resisted marriage and had yet to start a family obscures the fact that he was already 34 years old by the time he appeared in his first movie. The relative brevity of his film career should not be held as a criticism of his acting but instead as an indicator of the importance of his stage career. While everyone is aware of Astaire's achievements on screen, it is often forgotten that his career as a stage performer lasted longer than his time as a film actor. For Astaire, screen acting was for the most part a middle-aged pursuit, making his dancing performances on screen all the more remarkable.

Even though Astaire was signed by RKO in 1933, his first film was not with his parent studio but instead with MGM. In a sense, it was fitting that his first film, *Dancing Lady*, should be produced by MGM, because that studio remains the one most closely associated with the musical, and Astaire is the film star still inextricably linked with the musical. At the same time, RKO had a clear rationale for loaning their new actor, because Astaire's role was minor and he appeared as himself. The plot, which involves Joan Crawford's character attempting to leave her job as a stripper and join forces with a stage director (played by Clark Gable), is clearly a vehicle for Crawford and Gable. Nevertheless, the film was an ideal opening film for Astaire, because having him to appear as himself allowed him to ease into the new medium. Writer G. Bruce Boyer wrote over half a century later, "I think I can pinpoint the one moment when the American style of dressing first appeared. It was in an appalling 1933 movie called Dancing Lady during an otherwise forgettable dance number. It also just happened to be Fred Astaire's first on-camera dance. But don't look at the steps. Look at the outfit: Astaire is wearing a single-breasted, soft flannel suit with two-tone spectator shoes and a turtleneck. You wish you could look that stylish! Later that year, in Flying Down to Rio, we get the full Astaire impact. The muted plaid suit is not all that striking, but Fred is wearing it with a soft button-down shirt, a pale woven tie, silk pocket square, bright horizontally striped hose and white bucks. Whoa! Now that's different. This melange of the classic and the sporty was an American innovation. As we approach the impeccable Astaire's 100th birthday on May 10, it's worth remembering that he remains the greatest exemplar of that style."

Meanwhile, when Rogers arrived in Hollywood, she was hardly a major star. Her fame had been acquired through Broadway rather than cinema, and while she had appeared in several films for Paramount, her roles were relatively minor and the films were not blockbusters. Her first contract in Hollywood was with RKO Pathe, the studio for which she would later act with Fred Astaire. The contract was for three films, all released between 1931 and 1932: *The Tip-Off* (1931), *Suicide Fleet* (1932), and *Carnival Boat* (1932). The three films, all of which were directed by Albert Rogell, were very low-budget productions and did little to advance her reputation.

After the contract ended, Rogers began oscillating between studios, appearing in substantial roles but relegated to B-movies. One of her films from 1932, *The Thirteenth Guest*, is a representative example of the types of films she appeared in during her earliest years in Hollywood. She stars as Marie Morgan, a woman who must fend off death at a dinner party. The film is a classic example of a B-movie horror film, precisely the sort of film that was included in a double feature alongside a more glossy production. It was produced by Monogram Pictures Corporation, a small-scale studio that specialized in low-budget horror films. In sum, the film padded Rogers's resume but would not have any major effect in leading to her receiving more substantial roles.

Ginger's first major film role would not be with RKO but instead with Warner Brothers, when she was cast in the musical, *42nd Street* (1933). At the time that the film was being cast, she had been dating Mervyn Leroy, the famous director who was responsible for gangster films such as *I Am a Fugitive from a Chain Gang* (1932). Leroy was the original director and was replaced after falling ill, but his involvement with the film's production led to Rogers being cast in the role. The moderately racy plot featured two Broadway producers who subsidize a musical, and behind-the-scenes intrigue takes place as the main star is romantically involved with the man responsible for financially backing the production. Rogers appears as "Anytime Annie," a chorus girl with loose morals. Eventually, the show-within-a-film becomes a major success, and *42nd Street* also performed well at the box office.

Mervyn Leroy

Ginger in *42nd Street*

While the plot of *42nd Street* is contextually relevant and contained many elements of 1920s America, including flappers, gangsters, and financial anxieties associated with the Great

Depression, it was not the plot of the film that made the movie a commercial success. Rather, there is a strict separation between the musical numbers and the narrative, with the musical productions under the direction of famed choreographer Busby Berkeley. Infamous for his lavish set designs, rapid camera editing, and scantily-clad actresses, Berkeley's films were incredibly popular during the Great Depression. The blatant escapism of the plots, with their clear divide between the anxieties of the cultural moment and the glory of the musical numbers, appealed to an American public that needed relief (however temporary) from the turmoil of the Great Depression. The frantic editing of the camera and lavish configurations of chorus girls also makes the films worthy for their virtuoso technical achievements, as one of the great appeals to Berkeley films was simply gazing in wonderment at the seemingly impossible feats achieved by Berkeley with his camera. *42nd Street* was nominated for an Academy Award for Best Picture and one for Best Sound Recording, and it grossed over $2 million at the box office as well. In the end, films such as *42nd Street* had a palliative effect on the audience, and while they are perhaps difficult to appreciate for a 21st century audience, they performed a valuable function during early 1930s.

Berkeley

Building upon the success of *42nd Street*, Rogers's next significant film was another Berkeley picture, *Gold Diggers of 1933* (1933). The film was even more garish than *42nd Street* and stands as perhaps the most representative example of Berkeley's style. The musical numbers are not well-integrated into the plot, as the film literally pauses for minutes on end in order to accompany Berkeley's technical virtuosity with the camera, and the innumerable chorus girls perform in outfits that blatantly objectify them. *Gold Diggers of 1933* is a prime example of the lax nature of the early years of the Hays Code's censorship. While the Hays Code was technically adopted in 1930, it would be roughly four years before it was enforced in any serious manner, and films such as *Gold Diggers* were able to gain approval despite their racy subject matter. Rogers stars as Fay Fortune, a woman who is interested only in money, making her one of the money-seeking women referred to by the film's title. As with *42nd Street*, the film centers on the production of the show, with the chief financial backer doubling as the main romantic lead. Rogers was not cast as the leading actress (a role performed by Ruby Keeler), but she plays a prominent role in the most famous musical number in the film (one of four numbers in the film designed by Berkeley), a rendition of "We're in the Money." Performed by an enormous collection of showgirls, Rogers performs a verse of the song herself in Pig Latin. The musical number is obviously designed to objectify her (as evidenced by her suggestive outfit), but she also reveals her singing and dancing talents. Peter Williams Evans notes that the garish quality of her performances in the Berkeley films demonstrated how Rogers possessed a boldness that was suppressed in her later films: "Rogers's early Warner Brothers musical appearances as Anytime Annie in *42nd Street* and Fay Fortune in *Gold Diggers of 1933* draw attention, through her characters' names, to the sort of wrong-side-of-the-tracks parts in which she flourished…The brassy prankster lurks beneath the wide-eyed ingénue that she was called on to play in the later RKO films with Astaire." (29).

Rogers in *Gold Diggers of 1933*

The ham-fisted nature of Ginger's two films with Busby Berkeley was essentially the antithesis of her later films with Fred Astaire, and one of the great ironies of her career is that it was her performances in the Berkeley films that revealed that she possessed the skills needed to appear alongside Fred Astaire.

While the Berkeley films were the most noteworthy, that hardly scratches the surface of just how busy Ginger Rogers was during her early years as a film actress. She performed in an astonishing 10 films during 1933 alone. Certainly, it was not unusual for actresses during that time to appear in several films per year (particularly B-pictures, which were often completed in a manner of weeks), but her workload is remarkable even when viewed through the lens of her contemporary moment. Perhaps unsurprisingly, Rogers's second husband happened to be a co-star of hers. In 1934, she married Lew Ayres, who had starred alongside her in *Don't Bet on Love* (1933). But almost from the beginning of the marriage, the relationship was compromised by the fact that neither was willing to sacrifice their career in the interest of the marriage, and they separated in 1936. They would remain married for seven years but would not have any children.

Lew Ayres

Chapter 4: The Fred and Ginger Musicals

"Believe me, Ginger was great. She contributed her full fifty percent in making them such a great team. She could follow Fred as if one brain was thinking. She blended with his every step and mood immaculately. He was able to do dances on screen that would have been impossible to risk if he hadn't had a partner like Ginger - as skillful as she was attractive." – Edward Everett Horton

Even though *Don't Bet on Love* showcased Ginger with her future husband, the film was hardly the most significant of the year for Rogers. After all, 1933 was the year in which Rogers starred with Fred Astaire for the first time, as the two appeared together in *Flying Down to Rio*. The film features Fred and Ginger as Fred Ayres and Honey Hale, a band leader and star vocalist for the same orchestra, but the plot is little more than a thinly veiled opportunity to showcase the bravura dancing theatrics of Astaire and Rogers. In a way, Astaire might as well have been playing himself in the film, and his character's initials are the same as his own. As *Variety* magazine wrote in a review, "The main point of Flying Down to Rio is the screen promise of Fred Astaire ... He's assuredly a bet after this one, for he's distinctly likable on the screen, the mike is kind to his voice and as a dancer he remains in a class by himself. The latter observation will be no news to the profession, which has long admitted that Astaire starts dancing where the others stop hoofing."

Although that review recognized Astaire and was proof that he was better known as a dancer by that point, one of the more compelling aspects of the film is that Rogers was billed ahead of Astaire, the only film in which this occurs. In 1934, Rogers was a more prominent film star than her now famous co-star, and there is a way in which the trajectory of their working relationship reflects the usurping of Rogers by Astaire. Of course, as Edward Gallafent notes, there was no way that RKO could have ever predicted that the two would evolve into the Fred and Ginger pairing: "The status of *Flying Down to Rio* as marking the opening of the Astaire-Rogers cycle is purely retrospective: its audience and its producers could not know of the films to come with which we associate it, and if conditions had arisen to prevent the making of another movie between these two actors, there would be no light thrown on it by the rest of the cycle." (12)

Not only was there no way for the audience and producers to know at the time of *Flying Down to Rio* that Fred Astaire and Ginger Rogers would evolve into arguably the most famous pairing in film history, but the film's plotline gives no indication either. Indeed, one of the most jarring aspects of the films is simply watching Fred and Ginger as supporting actors. As a result, the film is notably less romantic than their later films, with "the idea of sexual attachment between them never explicitly raised, the matter of romance and particularly of a first encounter between lovers being assigned to the principal couple" (Gallafent 16). In the film, Astaire and Rogers perform together in four musical numbers, including the title song, "Orchids in Moonlight," and "Music Makes Me." *Flying Down to Rio* was a moderate success, but it grossed nowhere near the sums that the later Astaire-Rogers films would garner. Even so, it was clear that RKO had a winning formula; audiences might have been familiar with Astaire's dancing on stage, but they had never been privy to such dancing on the screen, and RKO simply possessed a commodity that no other studio could match.

Moreover, Astaire and Rogers displayed an intuitive chemistry that made it seem as though they had performed together for years. Of course, the chemistry was the result of plenty of hard work, as Rogers noted, "How do you think those routines were accomplished? With mirrors?... Well, I thought I knew what concentrated work was before I met Fred, but he's the limit. Never satisfied until every detail is right, and he will not compromise. No sir! What's more, if he thinks of something better after you've finished a routine, you do it over."

Astaire and Rogers in *Flying Down to Rio*

In 1934, Astaire famously wrote to his agent, "What's all this talk about me being teamed with Ginger Rogers? I will not have it Leland--I did not go into pictures to be teamed with her or anyone else, and if that is the program in mind for me I will not stand for it. I don't mind making another picture with her but as for this teams idea, it's out." But of course, pairing Astaire with Ginger Rogers was obviously a wise decision, as the chemistry between the two is beyond reproach. When conceiving of the tandem, it is common to think of Astaire as the dominant figure, and indeed Astaire was the far more accomplished dancer. At the same time, however, Rogers was significantly more experienced as a film actress, as she had broken into Hollywood in 1929. There was no way that RKO could possibly supply Astaire with a dance partner who could match his abilities, but Rogers was an ideal fit since she was an adept dancer in her own right and also possessed the acting skills and glamorous physical appearance required of a leading actress. As Katharine Hepburn would later note of Astaire and Rogers, "He gives her class and she gives him sex appeal." Each supplied the other with a necessary missing ingredient for film stardom.

After *Flying Down to Rio*, Ginger's contract with RKO was renewed, and after appearing in several films in late 1933 and early 1934, she and Astaire were cast in a second film together, *The Gay Divorcee* (1934). She received $1100 per week for the film, a sum that was scarcely higher than her salary on Broadway several years earlier. However, while Ginger's early years in Hollywood were not particularly lucrative when compared with her stage career, *The Gay Divorcee* played an integral role in continuing to build the popularity of the Fred and Ginger pairing. The film was blessed by the fact that Astaire starred in the stage version of the film, and viewers quickly get the sense the part was tailor-made for him. He stars as Guy Holden, a professional dancer, while Rogers stars as a frustrated wife looking to obtain a divorce. The film is a prominent example of the manner in which Astaire was typically cast as an entertainer while

Rogers appears in more "ordinary" roles. *The Gay Divorcee* represents the film that effectively reversed the dynamic between Astaire and Rogers, and from that point forward, he would represent the dominant figure in the pairing. Highlighted by the Astaire-Rogers performance of "Night and Day," the film was nominated for several Academy Awards, including Best Picture.

One of the under-recognized aspects of the Fred and Ginger relationship is that even while they appeared together throughout the 1930s, their careers were substantially different. Indeed, while Astaire appeared in just one film without Ginger during the 1930s, Rogers was required to appear in numerous films in between the famous musicals. In fact, it was not until 1936 that she appeared in consecutive films with Fred Astaire. In fairness to RKO, the easy impulse to chastise the studio for requiring Rogers to appear in more films than Astaire is not entirely fair. In between films, Astaire remained quite busy, and he was responsible for designing the musical numbers for the following film, a task he completed with good friend Hermes Pan. Thus, Astaire and Rogers each remained busy in between their films together, despite the fact that it appeared as though Rogers was being worked more severely than her co-star.

Between *The Gay Divorcee* and her next film with Fred Astaire, Rogers appeared in *Romance in Manhattan*, a comedy that paired her with Stephen Roberts. Unlike the Astaire-Rogers musicals, the film has a strong realist bent, portraying the plight of an impoverished Czech immigrant as he attempts to earn a living during the Great Depression. Rogers is cast as a showgirl who eventually marries the immigrant. The film exposes the irony involved in the fact that it was the non Astaire-Rogers films that more frequently cast Ginger as a musical entertainer, while the more famous Fred and Ginger films often featured her as an everywoman who becomes indoctrinated into the world of musical performing through her relationship with Astaire's character.

The third Fred and Ginger musical was *Roberta*, an adaptation of a Broadway musical from two years prior. Astaire plays a performer with a dance band, Huck Haines, who travels to Paris with his friend and unexpectedly meets his hometown girlfriend, Liz, who has become famous as Countess Scharwenka. The romance between the Astaire-Rogers couple occurs through the production of a fashion show Huck's friend is tasked with producing. Setting the film in Paris allowed the film to juxtapose the European snobbery personified by the secondary female lead, Stephanie (played by Irene Dunn), with the down-to-earth personality of Ginger Rogers. Sarah Berry notes that the ability to combine elements of high and popular culture makes the film a representative example of the film musical genre: "The film's musical sequences with Fred Astaire and Ginger Rogers contrast with Stephanie's aristocratic style, providing the synthesis of high and low culture that characterizes many Hollywood musicals. Rogers's masquerade as Scharwenka both lampoons the implied superiority of European aristocrats and makes Rogers's character a mixture of "real" American earthiness and "put-on" glamour. Astaire's Huck combines American popular culture with simple, well-suited elegance." (67). This reading of *Roberta* applies to many of the Astaire-Rogers films, identifying how one of her great accomplishments was her ability to appear glamorous without exuding a hint of snobbery. In so doing, Ginger came across as glamorous and sophisticated without also seeming pretentious in a way that characterized European transplants like Greta Garbo and Marlene Dietrich.

As with *The Divorcee* (as well as the later Astaire-Rogers movies), one of the most notable aspects of the film is the way in which there is no clear divide separating the musical numbers from the rest of the plot. The romance between the two major stars is directly embedded within the plot, rather than existing outside of it, as was common during the time period. To this end, it is important to note that the major model for the film musical during the first five years of synchronized sound was the style popularized by Busby Berkeley. In Berkeley's films, the plot itself is flimsy and essentially accomplishes little other than filling time between the lavish, fantastical musical productions. In fact, on many of his films, Berkeley designed only the musical sequences, with a separate director in charge of the rest of the plot.

In contrast with that style, when watching the Fred and Ginger films, viewers do not feel as though the narrative has been paused for the musical numbers. On a formal level, this effect is achieved through the differences in camera technique that separate their films; where Astaire's musical numbers were always conveyed through a single shot, Berkeley deployed kaleidoscopic montages, splicing up the scene into an array of images that occasionally cause an aesthetic overload. Discussing the use of a single shot with a camera later called the "Astaire dolly", producer H.C. Dolley explained, "It was on tiny wheels with a mount for the camera that put the lens about two feet above the ground. On it rode the camera operator and the assistant who changed the focus and that's all. Fred always wanted to keep the camera in as tight as possible, and they used to shoot with a 40 millimeter lens, which doesn't give you too much leeway. So every time Fred and Ginger moved toward us, the camera had to go back, and every time they went back, the camera went in. The head grip who was in charge of pushing this thing was a joy to watch. He would maintain a consistent distance, and when they were in the midst of a hectic dance that's quite a stunt."

Expounding on the differences between Astaire and Berkeley is necessary since the two would remain rivals throughout the decade. Historically, it has been common to argue that Astaire's model for the film musical usurped that of Berkeley, but this was hardly the case. Astaire's films may have been more popular, but Berkeley continued to offer an alternative model for the genre. Andrew Sarris explains the actual dynamic between Astaire and Berkeley that existed during the 1930s: "It is customary for film historians to assume that Busby Berkeley's style of mass choreography and aerial cinematography were completely eclipsed by the relative grace and simplicity of the Fred Astaire-Ginger Rogers musicals. Actually, Berkeley and Astaire overlapped and coexisted as stylistic alternatives for the Hollywood musical to follow." (172) Thus, while it is impossible to deny that Astaire's musical style became the dominant method on film, Berkeley remained in Hollywood even while Astaire eclipsed his popularity, and the differences between the two musical styles demonstrate there were multiple elements of the musical as a genre.

Fred and Ginger in *Roberta*

Building on the success of *Roberta*, Astaire and Rogers made arguably their most famous film later that same year. *Top Hat* (1935) is routinely listed among the most successful in the genre, and it included some of the most famous Astaire-Rogers musical numbers. In addition, the success of the film can also be attributed to the allure of the plot, which consists of Astaire as a dancer traveling abroad in London. He falls in love with Rogers, who plays a professional model. The narrative involves a case of mistaken identity that is eventually reconciled, culminating with Astaire and Rogers agreeing to marry. A number of famous musical numbers are included, including Astaire and Roger together in "Cheek to Cheek" and Astaire by himself in "No Strings I'm Fancy Free" and "Top Hat, White Tie, and Tails." The latter number was responsible for establishing the top hat and coat tails that are associated with the Astaire image. The film was truly the ideal vehicle for Astaire, as no other film offered him so many ideal opportunities to showcase his dancing technique.

Astaire and Rogers at the climax of "Cheek to Cheek"

Of course, the success of *Top Hat* not only resulted from Astaire's dancing but also his chemistry with Ginger Rogers and the general appeal of the plot. The dancing sequences are not a narrative digression (in the Busby Berkeley tradition) but instead serve as a form of courtship. In an age in which the Hays Code restricted romantic activity, Astaire's dancing signifies his sexual potency, while Rogers's ability to hang with him during long, complicated sequences suggests that she is capable of satisfying his romantic desires and serving as his wife. The film thus managed to be very romantic (if not sexy) without ever showing its two stars engaged in explicitly sexual activity. In this regard, Sue Rickard explains, Whether the number advances the narrative or not, emotional energies are heightened by the music, creating the possibility of a more intense spectatorial identification with the images on screen. Under these circumstances it is not difficult to interpret many of the Astaire/Rogers dances as displaced sexual activity." (75). The belief that the dazzling musical numbers constituted a means of circumventing the Hays Code is substantiated by the fact that Astaire is undeniably far sexier while performing his dance routines than during the rest of the narrative. Explaining why this is the case, Rickard argues that even though he did not possess a traditionally masculine physique, Astaire's "mastery of the body" transformed him into figure worthy of female desire." (80)

The plot of *Top Hat* is also notable for representing what Rick Altman refers to as the "fairy tale musical," one of three categories that Altman identifies for the musical genre. In the fairy tale musical, the formation of the romantic couple is framed in such a way that the romantic leads appear predestined to fall in love, with their romance forming a private kingdom of sorts (Altman). As Altman clarifies, this subgenre is indebted to opera: "The fairy tale musical, first of the three subgenres to reach maturity in film, did so thanks to massive borrowing from a long tradition of European and American operettas. While the history of the Hollywood fairy tale musical reveals numerous attempts to 'Americanize' the pattern established in nineteenth-century European operetta, it must nevertheless be admitted that the fairy tale musical on film is part of a tradition that begins long before cinema." (131)

Altman's description identifies salient elements associated with Astaire individually and the musical genre as a whole. Specifically, the high-class nature of European opera fed seamlessly into the image that Astaire had first cultivated during his stage career; ever since his first trip to Europe as a dancer alongside Adele, Fred had been enraptured by the high culture elements of European society, and the fairy tale musical was the ideal model through which to project the cultured, high society image he wished to exude. On a broader level, the many Astaire-Rogers fairy tale musicals popularized the subgenre. They were hardly the first examples of the fairy tale musical genre in Hollywood, but the chemistry between Astaire and Rogers brought the form to greater popularity than it had previously enjoyed.

For all of the glamour of the setting, one of the dominant themes raised by *Top Hat* is the juxtaposition between the very ordinary nature of Fred Astaire's character (and the plot more generally) and the spectacular nature of the dances between Astaire and Rogers. Perhaps more than any other film in the Fred and Ginger oeuvre, the film exposes the awkwardness of Fred Astaire when not dancing. His timidity around Ginger Rogers's character is the polar opposite of the confident dancing master who awes the audience with each dance sequence. Moreover, he is physically no match for Rogers; even in an era in which male actors were far shorter than they would later become, Astaire is not as stereotypically masculine as contemporary actors such as Spencer Tracy and Clark Gable. His balding hairline was partially remedied through wearing hairpieces, but even with such cosmetic enhancements, no one would justifiably consider him a leading man based on his physical attributes. Where Rogers' tall, blonde physique made her the archetypal leading woman for 1930s Hollywood, Astaire superficially appeared an unlikely match.

With the success of *Top Hat*, Astaire and Rogers rose to the top of the Hollywood elite, and while most actors relatively new to Hollywood are forced to appear in numerous films per year, Astaire was granted the privilege of appearing in no more than two. This arrangement gave him plenty of time to rehearse for his parts, and he was also given the leeway to alter his parts as he saw fit. Meanwhile, Rogers was far more active, regularly working on pictures for RKO. Rogers would later note, "We were only together for a part of my career, and for every film we did, I did another three on my own. The studio was working me too hard. Fred would rush off for a holiday and call me and say: 'Hey, ready to do another?' And I didn't have the sense to say that I was too tired. Those times were murder for me. Oh, I adored Mr. A but all the hard work...the 5 a.m. calls, the months of non-stop dancing, singing and acting. We just worked it out and had a lot of fun and got very exhausted. And Mr. A was quite divine."

Astaire and Rogers in *Top Hat*

From a technical standpoint, *Top Hat* is considered one of the most impressive of the Astaire-Rogers films. The film was nominated for several Academy Awards, including Best Picture, Art Direction, Original Song, and Dance Direction. Several of the musical numbers are recognized as among the most successful in the genre, and the structure of the numbers set the dynamic for many of Astaire and Rogers's later films. For example, Astaire dances a solo number early in the film, as he would with their later films. In addition, the romance between Astaire and Rogers is conveyed through dance, with Rogers proving that she can match her male co-star's physical virtuosity. At the start of the film, Astaire's dancing appears almost otherworldly, yet by the film's conclusion, Rogers proves that she is an adept dancer and the Fred and Ginger romantic grouping is solidified.

The difference in Astaire's image between his "regular" self and his dancing self foregrounds the spectacular nature of the Fred and Ginger musical numbers, with their dances transforming everyday reality into an almost magical fantasy space. The dream-like nature of numbers such as "Cheek to Cheek" (in *Top Hat*) make the Fred and Ginger musicals perhaps the most iconic examples of Rick Altman's theory of the "fairy tale musical" (155). Listed as one of three subcategories in Altman's taxonomy of the film musical, the fairy tale musical takes as its premise the belief that the formation of the romantic couple is achieved through song and dance, resulting in the "restoration of order to an imaginary kingdom" (126).

As Altman notes the fairy tale musical borrows heavily from the European opera, allowing Fred and Ginger musicals such as *Top Hat* to caricature European high society, a motif that also was on display in *Roberta*. Meanwhile, the "imaginary kingdom" established through the fairy tale musical identifies the manner in which fairy tale musicals (*Top Hat* being arguably the best example) tie the romantic plot to a transformation of everyday reality.

One similarity between films such as *Top Hat* and those of Busby Berkeley is that both provided a morale boost to an American public that was in the throes of the Great Depression. Viewers could revel in the spectacular camera feats of films such as *Gold Diggers of 1933*, or they could delight in the physicality displayed by Rogers and Astaire in their films. The major difference is that the Fred and Ginger films amazed viewers through the talents of the actors, while the Berkeley films are remarkable for the talents of the technology and craft of the director. According to Annette Kuhn, the approach undertaken by the Astaire-Rogers pictures resonated more strongly with contemporary viewers: "The more integrated the musical, the greater becomes the potential for the themes or the address of its numbers to engage with audiences' lives, inner as well as outer, beyond the cinema. In these respects, the films of Fred Astaire and Ginger Rogers, all of them integrated musicals, are of considerable cultural significance." (169).

Kuhn's explanation of the integrated musical and its cultural importance is perhaps overblown, but there is no doubting that the narrative integration of the Fred and Ginger films proved to be box office gold, with viewers easily able to identify with the principal characters. Naturally, as the 1930s progressed, the ratio between Ginger's films with Fred Astaire and the other movies she made for RKO tilted predominantly toward the former. Given the box office success of the Fred and Ginger films, RKO began allowing Rogers to appear in fewer films per year than she had earlier in the decade, and in 1936 she campaigned for a higher salary, a request that was entirely reasonable in light of the fact that she not only earned less than Astaire but was also paid less than the secondary male actors in the films she appeared in with Astaire. Rogers was arguably the most prominent star in Hollywood, and yet she was treated as though she were a contract player. She was finally awarded a higher salary, a development that coincided with her less strenuous workload.

After *Top Hat*, Rogers appeared in one film without Astaire, *In Person* (1935), a minor film that paired her with 1930s leading man George Brent. The film was not particularly successful from either a commercial or critical standpoint. Meanwhile, the critical and commercial successes Astaire enjoyed in 1936 corresponded with similarly positive changes in his personal life. That same year, Astaire and his wife, Phyllis, had their first child, Fred Jr., who was born on New Year's Day. Six years later, in March of 1942, Phyllis would give birth to a second child, Ava Ashire McKenzie. With two kids, one boy and one girl, the Astaires embodied the American Dream, and for all the high-class trappings associated with his top hat and coat tails, Astaire led a quiet private life in California. During a time in which Hollywood was filled with left-wing political activists, Astaire was a Republican (although not an outspoken one), and it is no exaggeration to state that he was a social conservative as well. Instead of expressing political critiques in his films, the Astaire movies were predicated solely toward showcasing his dazzling dancing techniques.

From 1936-1937, Astaire and Rogers starred in three consecutive films with each other: *Follow the Fleet* (1936), *Swing Time* (1936), and *Shall We Dance* (1937). The films built on the success of the early Fred and Ginger films while also pointing their themes in new directions. Of these, *Shall We Dance* (1937) was the most famous. In a major feat for the studio, RKO was able to secure George and Ira Gershwin to score the film, reuniting Astaire with one of his favorite collaborators from his stage career. The film did not bring the commercial or critical success of the earlier Fred and Ginger pictures, but working with the Gershwins was an example of how fortunate Astaire was to collaborate with musical luminaries. To this end, Epstein astutely contends, "A good measure of the success behind the Astaire-Rogers partnership is also owed to the fact that they came together at a time when an extraordinary clutch of great songwriters were at work" (xviii).

Of the three films Astaire and Rogers appeared in together between 1936 and 1937, *Follow the Fleet* was the most commercially successful yet received the most lukewarm critical response. The film's strong box office numbers were perhaps an inevitable result of the public's love for *Top Hat*, but the plot of *Follow the Fleet* is often confusing and cumbersome. Even so, the film is nevertheless worthy of watching, above all because it revealed Ginger's substantial improvements as a dancer (Croce). In dance sequences such as "Let's Face the Music and Dance," it is Rogers' dancing that nearly steals the spotlight from her male co-star. To this end, it is worth remembering that at the start of the Astaire-Rogers pairing, Rogers had a developed singing voice but was still relatively inexperienced as a dancer. One of the reasons that the couple were so successful together was that their strengths complemented one another so seamlessly - Astaire's dancing ability compensated for Rogers' deficiency, while her singing made up for Astaire's relative lack of singing ability. While Astaire's singing never improved in any significant sense, with *Follow the Fleet* Rogers revealed that she could dance at an expert level.

Astaire and Rogers's second film in 1936, *Swing Time*, is considered by many to be their finest film together. The film's plot features Astaire as "Lucky" Garnett, a dancer who doubles as a gambler. The complicated, screwball plot involves Lucky's attempt to earn enough money to persuade his fiancées father that he possesses enough money to adequately provide for his future spouse. His attempts to raise money result in him meeting Penny (played by Ginger Rogers), a piano instructor, and eventually they fall in love, with their dancing sequences facilitating the growth of their burgeoning romance. At the same time, the film is notably less sophisticated in tone than *Top Hat*, and while one could still argue that it qualifies as a fairy tale musical, it does not offer the European polish of the earlier film. This important contrast between *Top Hat* and *Swing Time* reveals how while many might consider the canon of Fred and Ginger films to have a strong degree of continuity, there are significant differences between them. In this regard, Arlene Croce contends that there is a call-and-response dynamic between their films, such that each new Fred and Ginger film commented on motifs of earlier ones. *Swing Time* is perhaps the best example of this tendency, as it serves as a counterpoint to the glossy sophistication of the earlier film.

As Croce's argument suggests, *Swing Time* is not as sophisticated in nature as *Top Hat*. Both films showcase remarkable dancing sequences (indeed, with Rogers's improvements, the dance sequences in the later film are even more impressive), yet *Swing Time* includes scenes that are almost campy in nature. One example of this tendency is Astaire's solo performance in the film, "Bojangles of Harlem," which depicts the famous actor in blackface and wearing stilts. In addition, the plot includes elements that are highly comedic, placing Astaire and Rogers in a zany plot. In her analysis of the chemistry between Astaire and Rogers, Martha Nochimson claims that the Fred and Ginger pairing was so appealing since they form a counterpoint to a world filled with chaos, an interpretation that deviates sharply from the traditional stance that Rogers supplied the sex appeal and Astaire brought sophisticated dancing proficiency: "The actual content of these films stands in direct opposition to the reductive, oft-repeated bromide coined by Katharine Hepburn: 'He gave her class; she gave him sex.' Indeed, far from fitting the clichéd gender categories within where the male guarantees status and the female provides the sensual attraction, at their best, the Astaire and Rogers figures are defined by the way they do not fit stereotypes. They oppose a farcical and manufactured culture with an organic energy that comes from their bodies but does not easily find expression within the social maze of confusion." (139).

Swing Time is the most representative example of Nochimson's argument. Just as the fairy tale musical involves Rogers and Astaire forming a kingdom that secludes them from their everyday environment, Nochimson's outline positions the formation of the romantic couple as a means of transcending the chaotic nature of everyday reality. This juxtaposition between the idyllic romantic grouping against the unstructured outside world also aligns the Astaire and Rogers musicals with the screwball comedy, a genre that was especially prevalent during the 1930s and would ultimately culminate with Howard Hawks' *Bringing Up Baby* (1938) and *His Girl Friday* (1940). Indeed, the physical sparring between Astaire and Rogers (with each proving that they could dance as well as the other) is the physical equivalent of the verbal sparring that occurred in the most famous screwball comedy films. Ultimately, films such as *Swing Time* prove that it is most accurate to refer to the Astaire-Rogers films not as musicals but rather as musical-comedies.

Astaire and Rogers in *Swing Time*

Ginger's non-Astaire film from 1937 was *Stage Door*, a film that paired her with Katharine Hepburn, her great rival at RKO throughout the 1930s. Off the movie set, the two were major rivals, with the Republican, Christian Scientist Rogers contrasting with the ultra-liberal Hepburn. Throughout most of the decade, Rogers had dominated their rivalry, with Hepburn being recognized as a box office pariah at around the time that *Stage Door* was made. Over the next several years, Hepburn would effectively usurp Rogers in Hollywood, and one of the interesting subtexts of the film is that it showcases the two actresses shortly before Hepburn would leap past Rogers in the eyes of the public. In the film, Rogers and Hepburn star as roommates who cannot get along with one another, although at the end of the film they overcome their differences. The film did not earn as much at the box office as *Shall We Dance*, but it received favorable reviews from the critical establishment and earned an Academy Award Nomination for Best Picture.

The final films in which Astaire starred with Rogers during the decade were *Carefree* (1938) and *The Story of Vernon and Irene Castle* (1939). As always, the two films benefitted from the skilled performances of the two stars, but as Astaire and Rogers grew in fame, it became increasingly difficult to generate a substantial profit. Not only did Fred and Ginger command a lofty salary for each picture, it cost a great deal of money to secure the talents of the other members of the production team. As a result, even though the two films performed well at the box office, they each lost money for the studio due to the immense production costs.

One of the most compelling aspects of the Fred and Ginger films from the end of the 1930s is that they forecast the demise of the famous pairing. Their 1938 film, *Carefree*, includes just four musical numbers and features Astaire and Rogers in the unlikely roles of psychiatrist and patient respectively. Even though the film was nominated for three Academy Awards, it was a box office failure. Making matters worse, RKO began to realize that the box office totals were becoming inversely proportionate to the amount spent on the films. Musicals are inherently expensive to produce, and as they began spending more and more on the Fred and Ginger films, the films began grossing incrementally smaller totals.

The final musical Rogers appeared in with Astaire during the 1930s was *The Story of Vernon and Irene Castle* (1939), a film that clearly signals that the end of the famous pairing was imminent. Set at the outbreak of World War I, the film features Rogers as an American dancer who attempts to convince vaudeville comedian Vernon Castle (played by Astaire) to become a ballroom dancer. However, Vernon is called upon to serve in the war, where he is killed. As Jane Feuer notes, the film is shocking to watch: "As Vernon and Irene, Astaire and Rogers seem to renounce the very star personas which had made the series a success. Astaire and Rogers no longer dance in their own special style…The songs are the standard tunes of that pre-World War One as opposed to the original contemporary scores of the series proper. Most shocking of all, the ineffable, immortal Fred Astaire dies at the end of the film." (98-99).

With its generic musical score, *The Story of Vernon and Irene Castle* might seem to be an ill-fitting conclusion to the remarkable run of success that Astaire and Rogers enjoyed. However, Feuer argues that by not appearing as another stereotypical Fred and Ginger film, the movie eased the American public into the post-Astaire-Rogers era, allowing them to see the famous pairing in a context divorced from their characteristically glamorous setting.

Chapter 5: Fred's Career after Ginger

"There comes a day when people begin to say, 'Why doesn't that old duffer retire?' I want to get out while they're still saying Astaire is a hell of a dancer." – Fred Astaire

Despite turning 40 in 1939, Astaire remained a box office draw, but the salaries commanded by Fred and Ginger made it unprofitable for them to continue to star alongside one another. Furthermore, Astaire was driven to pursue other opportunities, and he left RKO in 1939, reuniting with Rogers only on *The Barkleys of Broadway* (1949).

For better or worse, the films Astaire appeared in following his break with Ginger Rogers in 1939 are generally not well-remembered. However, even as he progressed into his middle-aged years, he remained active and danced at a high level. The first film he appeared in after leaving RKO was *Broadway Melody of 1940*, which paired him with Eleanor Powell, an actress with more dancing experience than Rogers had possessed at the start of her working relationship with Astaire. Despite being the only film in which Astaire would appear with Powell, the film remains noteworthy for the musical number "Begin the Beguine."

Astaire and Eleanor Powell in *Broadway Melody of 1940*

As the 1940s progressed, Astaire appeared alongside a wide array of co-stars. In 1941 and 1942, he appeared alongside a very young Rita Hayworth, who would become the most glamorous actress of the time period. The first of these films, *You'll Never Get Rich*, played a crucial role in facilitating Hayworth's rise to fame, and she would later state, "I guess the only jewels of my life were the pictures I made with Fred Astaire."

In the film, Astaire portrays a theater manager, making *You'll Never Get Rich* yet another example of the tendency for Astaire to portray characters employed in show business. The rationale behind his typecasting is easy to understand, since it helped the musical numbers fluidly integrate with the rest of the narrative. At the same time, it is worth considering whether Astaire was even capable of portraying other character types. After all, he did not possess a virile physique, and even in an era replete with relatively diminutive male stars like Humphrey Bogart and Spencer Tracy, Astaire's thin, balding appearance fell well short of the masculine model established by those actors.

Publicity image for *You'll Never Get Rich*

One major career development that occurred during the 1940s was that Astaire no longer occupied center stage in all of his films. Beginning with *Holiday Inn* in 1942, he was firmly relegated to the role of "co-star." In *Holiday Inn*, Astaire and Bing Crosby star as musical performers in a plot that charts the romances of Astaire with Virginia Dale and Crosby with Marjorie Reynolds, all set against the backdrop of the holiday season. The film is best remembered not for Astaire's contributions but instead for Bing Crosby's rendition of "White Christmas." Sharing the screen with a male co-star was difficult for Astaire, but he reunited with Crosby on *Blue Skies* (1946), an enormous box office success.

Holiday Inn

Despite the success of *Blue Skies*, Astaire was displeased with the film, and in a surprising decision, he announced his retirement later in 1946. The rationale behind the retirement was so that he could focus on his interests in horse racing, and while that was definitely a radical change, Astaire's slender physique and short height (about 5 foot 7 inches) made him small enough to be a natural jockey (Epstein). In addition, by 1946 he was already 47 years old, and he and Phyllis already had two children. Aside from his off-screen pursuits, the retirement was motivated by Fred's perception that his career was on the decline. For the first time in his career, he faced competition from Bing Crosby and Gene Kelly, both of whom were securing high-profile roles in Hollywood. Astaire thus had justifiable reasons for ending his film career, even if his retirement caught the public by surprise.

Astaire's retirement was relatively short-lived, as he returned to the screen after two years and starred in *Easter Parade* alongside Judy Garland in 1948. The film was a major success, and the unlikely pairing of Astaire and Garland paid dividends as they combined for numbers such as "The Ragtime Violin" and "Easter Parade." The film also benefited from the glossy treatment of MGM, with its sumptuous color punctuating the musical sequences. Despite remaining relatively unknown decades later, *Easter Parade* was the highest-grossing film of Astaire's career.

Over the next several years, Astaire continued to find steady acting opportunities with MGM, and the most acclaimed of Astaire's 1950s films was *The Band Wagon* (1953), directed by Vincente Minnelli. The film features Astaire in a semi-autobiographical role as Tony Hunter, an aging musical comedy star. In fact, one of the major motifs of the film consists of watching an aging Astaire growing old before the camera. In an early musical number, "Shine On Your Shoes," Astaire appears weathered and past his prime. However, the narrative revolves around Astaire proving that he can still succeed in the genre of musical comedy. Dana Polan argues that Astaire "changes from the aged Tony Hunter, has-been, into the graceful Fred Astaire whose every dance movement belies the passage of time. We watch Tony become not the artiste everyone wants him to be, but the song-and-dance man he once was" (141).

The film's most prominent musical number, "That's Entertainment," substantiates Polan's claim. Instead of promoting the production of *Oedipus Rex*, Astaire and his cohorts in the film revel in the joys of performing popular entertainment. Considering that Astaire had long projected a genteel aura, it is perhaps surprising to watch Astaire promote popular entertainment, but the film's celebration of performing song-and-dance routines correctly applies to Astaire's own life. Even though *The Band Wagon* was not a commercial success, it was nominated for a series of Academy Awards, including Best Music, and is routinely listed among Astaire's finest films.

Astaire in *The Band Wagon*

Astaire's productivity waned during the 1950s, a development due not only to his aging but also the death of his wife in 1954. Her death occurred suddenly, and Fred was unprepared for it; at the time of her death, he was busy acting in *Daddy Long Legs* (1955). After her death, he considered relinquishing his role on the film but then changed his mind. Unlike his earlier films from the decade, the film was not produced by MGM but instead by 20th Century Fox, as Astaire had been released from his studio contract two years earlier. The emergence of television was in the process of rendering cinema less profitable than it had been during the previous decade, but the musical remained relatively unscathed when compared with less glamorous genres.

Astaire in *Daddy Long Legs*

Daddy Long Legs was a significant film in Astaire's career for several reasons. First, it represented the first film in which he appeared that was produced in Cinemascope. The wide composition of the image afforded him with an expansive showcase for performing his dancing feats, and he captivates the screen in his role as a wealthy benefactor who becomes romantically involved with a French orphan. In addition to performing in Cinemascope for the first time, the film also marked the first of three Astaire films that were set in France. Two years later, he appeared in *Funny Face* (1957) with Audrey Hepburn. As with *Daddy Long Legs*, the film was one of the few in Astaire's career in which he did not play the role of a show business performer. Instead, he plays a fashion photographer who becomes enamored with Audrey Hepburn's character. The film, produced by Paramount, had an enormous budget, especially because Audrey Hepburn was perhaps the leading actress in Hollywood and famous fashion photographer Richard Avedon was hired to assist with the production. The film was a musical, and Astaire and Hepburn do dance together in the film, but the musical numbers were not integrated as tightly within the narrative as Astaire's earlier films with Ginger Rogers.

Astaire's final film, set in Paris, was *Silk Stockings* (1957), released in the same year as *Funny Face*. The film was a loose remake of Lubitch's famous *Ninotchka* (1939) and would be Fred's final musical of the 1950s. He played an American film producer, and apart from watching the 5 foot 7-inch Astaire dance alongside Cyd Charisse, the film remains noteworthy for "The Ritz of Rock and Roll," a musical number that spoofed rock and roll. Charisse would later speak at length about Astaire's dancing and compare it to Gene Kelly's, another prominent dancer who she performed with: "If I was black and blue, it was Gene. If I didn't have a scratch it was Fred." On another occasion, she expounded at length:

> "As one of the handful of girls who worked with both of those dance geniuses, I think I can give an honest comparison. In my opinion, Kelly is the more inventive choreographer of the two. Astaire, with Hermes Pan's help, creates fabulous numbers - for himself and his partner. But Kelly can create an entire number for somebody else... I think, however, that Astaire's coordination is better than Kelly's... his sense of rhythm is uncanny. Kelly, on the other hand, is the stronger of the two. When he lifts you, he lifts you!... To sum it up, I'd say they were the two greatest dancing personalities who were ever on screen. But it's like comparing apples and oranges. They're both delicious."

Astaire and Charisse in *The Bandwagon*

After *Silk Stockings*, Astaire did not retire, but his career went in new directions. First, he explored television for the first time, appearing in four television programs in which he performs dance routines. Indirectly, the television series returned Astaire to his early, pre-cinema stage career, where his dancing was no longer tied to a cinematic narrative but was the sole attraction. His dancing remained impressive even as he turned 60, and the program won Emmy Awards for

Best Performance by an Actor and Most Outstanding Single Program of the Year. Over the next couple of years, he appeared in other television programs, including a role in *It Takes a Thief* in 1968 and a number of made-for-television films.

One of the more surprising developments in Astaire's career was his decision at the end of the 1950s to begin appearing in films other than musicals. In 1959, he acted in *On the Beach*, a nuclear war film with an all-star cast that included not only Astaire but also Gregory Peck, Ava Gardner, and Anthony Perkins. The film led to other non-musical performances, including *The Pleasure of His Company* (1961) and *The Notorious Landlady* (1962). Astaire did return to the musical genre in 1968, appearing in Francis Ford Coppolla's *Finian's Rainbow*, but his final film was *Ghost Story* (1981), a horror film starring a long roster of aging stars, including John Houseman, Melvyn Douglas, and Douglas Fairbanks, Jr. The same year that *Ghost Story* was released, Astaire was awarded a Lifetime Achievement Award from the American Film Institute.

Astaire (right) in *On the Beach*

That Astaire's acting career continued well into old age reflects his excellent physical condition. Even when he was no longer able to dance on screen, he continued to act on a regular basis; *Ghost Story* was released when he was already in his 80s. His personal life also remained active well into old age. In 1980, Astaire married Robyn Smith, a horse jockey 45 years younger than himself. He and Smith had met through a mutual horse racing connection in 1973, and their marriage came after a long courtship. Fred continued to live in Beverley Hills and remained in strong health through his 80s until falling ill from pneumonia in 1989. He would die from the illness on June 22, having just turned 90 years old.

Chapter 6: Ginger's Career after Fred

"Ginger was brilliantly effective. She made everything work for her. Actually she made things very fine for both of us and she deserves most of the credit for our success." – Fred Astaire

With the Astaire and Rogers partnership over, Astaire broke from RKO and began freelancing. Meanwhile, Ginger remained under contract with her parent studio, and for the first time she began receiving top billing. The films she made without Astaire are for the most part largely forgotten, but it was ironically one of her post-Astaire films, *Kitty Foyle* (1940), that gave her the only Academy Award victory she would receive during her career. In a role that bore no resemblance to her earlier ones, she was cast in the title role as a saleswoman faced with the decision of either marrying a doctor or escaping with her romantic fling. The film unfolds in flashback structure, with a narrative trajectory that works its way back to the present, with her ultimately deciding to marry the doctor. The flashback structure was especially popular during the time period, and it would later become the dominant narrative device of film noir, even though that film itself is firmly positioned in the popular women's melodrama cycle of the late 1930s and 1940s. Although the film is ultimately conservative insofar as it promotes the patriarchal institution of marriage, by lending exposure to women's anxieties the film was designed to appeal to a female audience.

Rogers in *Kitty Foyle*

Off the movie set, the 1940s included many new developments for Rogers. In 1940, she purchased an enormous 1800 acre farm in Medford, Oregon. The farm produced fruit, dairy, and beef, and Rogers would spend an increasingly large amount of her time there over the years, eventually moving there permanently in her elderly years. After divorcing Lew Ayres, she married her next husband, Jack Briggs, in 1943. Briggs was a Marine Private who Rogers met while touring military bases. They married in January of 1943 shortly after having met, but the marriage was a disaster from the start, and they were separated by the end of July of that same year. Despite the marital discord, Rogers and Briggs would wait until 1949 before divorcing.

Throughout the 1940s, Rogers continued to appear in at least one film per year with the exception of 1948. Even though the departure of Katharine Hepburn made her RKO's most significant female star, Ginger also began appearing in films for other studios. Among the most notable were *Lady in the Dark* (1943), and the big-budget film *I'll Be Seeing You* (1944), which paired Rogers with Joseph Cotton and Shirley Temple. The latter film was particularly successful commercially, as Joseph Cotton's portrayal of the psychological effects of war resonated with the wartime audience. In 1945, she acted in *Week-End at the Waldorf*, which united Rogers with Lana Turner, Walter Pidgeon, and Van Johnson. The commercially successful film featured Rogers as a movie star who is one of many guests staying for a weekend at the Waldorf-Astoria hotel in New York City.

The most significant film Rogers appeared in during the late 1940s was *The Barkleys of Broadway* (1949), since it reunited her with Fred Astaire. Originally, the film was not intended to star Rogers because Judy Garland was under contract for the role, but her ongoing struggles with drug and alcohol addiction made her unavailable, so Rogers was signed for the part. The film portrays Astaire and Rogers as Josh and Dinah Barkley, a married couple that has reached success as a husband-and-wife team specializing in musical comedy. Dinah is approached with the possibility of starring in dramatic roles, and she secretly pursues the opportunity, threatening her marriage in the process. Eventually, she and her husband reconcile. The film produced the same blend of musical and screwball comedy that characterized films such as *Swing Time*, but it also ruminates on the more complex theme of high art (dramatic roles) versus popular art (musical comedy.) The film make the viewer appreciate the earlier Astaire-Rogers films all the more, particularly for the way that they managed to synthesize high and popular art, but there is also a novelty to *The Barkleys of Broadway*, not only for the interest of viewing Astaire and Rogers together at a more advanced age but also for the opportunity to view them in Technicolor. In any event, Fred and Ginger would not star alongside one another in any future films.

Fred and Ginger in *The Barkleys of Broadway*

With the arrival of the 1950s, Rogers's productivity began to wane, and like most actresses entering middle age, she found it more difficult to secure film roles. However, the decade also saw her bridge into a diverse array of film genres, including romantic comedies, family melodramas, and even thrillers. The most critically successful of these films was *Monkey Business* (1952), in which Rogers starred alongside Cary Grant and a young Marilyn Monroe. The plot featured her and Grant as a married couple whose lives have gone stale, but Grant's character works as a chemist and devises a potion that returns them to their youths. After taking the potion, they behave childishly, acting out their every impulse in a madcap spirit. Superficially, the plot suggests a rather infantile comedy, but as Robin Wood argues, the film offers a complex critique of bourgeois society and the difficulties involved in repressing one's savage urges: "If the descent into primitiveness of *Monkey Business* conveys a sense of dangerous uncontrol it conveys simultaneously a joyous exhilaration. Our primitive selves respond, our civilised selves tell us to be ashamed of the response: this is the tension that underlies *Monkey Business*, and Hawks here keeps the conflicting impulses perfectly in balance, without sacrifice of vitality." (77).

The film thus provokes an uneasy response from the viewer, who is at once tempted by the regressive behavior of the characters while also disgusted by their infantile behavior. Considering the success of the film, it is surprising that Rogers and Howard Hawks never collaborated again, but it's likely due to the fact Rogers was nearing the twilight of her Hollywood career and the opportunity did not present itself.

Rogers with Carey Grant and Marilyn Monroe in *Monkey Business*

In 1953, Rogers married Jacques Bergerac, a French lawyer she met while on a trip to Paris. The two had met one year prior, and after marrying they moved to Hollywood and Bergerac began a career of his own in the film industry. Yet again, the marriage did not last, and they would divorce in 1957. Rogers continued to star in films (albeit with less frequency) during the 1950s, but she was relegated to appearing in other genres. She starred in *Black Widow* (1954) and *Tight Spot* (1955), two late examples of the film noir genre. Subsequently, in 1956 Ginger starred in *Teenage Rebel*, a family melodrama that features Rogers as a divorced mother whose teenage daughter moves in to live with her for three weeks. Her last film of the decade was *Oh! Men, Oh! Women* (1957), after which she underwent an eight-year hiatus from acting in films. During this period, she remained active by returning to the theatre, appearing in at least one production per year from 1959-1965.

The 1960s also produced Ginger's final marriage, this time to film director and producer William Marshall. As with her earlier marriages, Rogers's relationship with her fifth husband was fraught with conflict; they remained married until divorcing in 1971, but Marshall's alcoholism made their marriage contentious. As happy as Rogers revealed herself to be to the public, her domestic life was filled with conflict throughout her adult life. All five of her marriages were major failures, and considering the conflict-ridden nature of her marriages, it is not surprising that Rogers never gave birth to any children in them.

Rogers returned to the screen twice in 1965. The first was William Dieterle's film *The Confession*, and her final performance was in *Harlow*, a biopic of actress Jean Harlow. Following her film career, she continued to maintain a prolific theatrical career. Two of her greatest stage successes were *Hello, Dolly* (1965) and *Mame* (1969). She would appear in a large number of productions of *Hello Dolly* over an 18-month period (Faris).

During the 1970s, Ginger served as a fashion consultant for J.C. Penney, and over the decade, she also hosted a musical revue, *The Ginger Rogers Show* (1975-80). Even in the 1980s, she continued to dance, with her final performance, *A Rockette Spectacular*, occurring in 1986. A late career highlight occurred in 1985, when she directed the stage musical *Babes in Arms*.

Ginger remained in good health through her 70s, continuing to live at her ranch in Oregon, but eventually she suffered a stroke that relegated her to a wheelchair. Despite that setback, she never bothered to see a doctor, and she died on April 25, 1995, with the official cause of death listed as a heart attack.

Chapter 7: The Legacy of Fred and Ginger

Fred Astaire's career spanned from 1905 through 1981, and the sheer length of it makes it possible to chart the developments that occurred in musical entertainment during the first three-quarters of the 20th century. Perhaps the most remarkable aspect of his career is that he managed to receive virtually unanimous acclaim. Referring to the reactions of cinematographers to the Astaire and Rogers movies, Annette Kuhn notes that Astaire and Rogers "are the only stars mentioned so often and…with such unanimous appreciation" (169). It is near impossible to encounter anyone who doesn't appreciate the films of Fred Astaire, and he managed to perform the seemingly impossible act of staying both critically acclaimed and beloved the entire time.

As unusual as Astaire's talent was, one of the more surprising aspects of his persona is the contrast between the extraordinary dancing feats he performed on screen and his relatively unremarkable physical appearance and personality off the movie set. A casual supporter of the Republican Party, Astaire preferred to distance himself from politics, and while many of his acting colleagues were embattled during the Red Scare, Astaire offered a comforting image of all-American conservatism. Similarly, during the Great Depression, Astaire enabled Americans to bask in the spectacle of his dancing feats with Ginger Rogers.

In the end, Astaire's overriding legacy can be found not so much in his films as the joy and entertainment he provided to America, and he continues to offer an idyllic model of entertainment divorced from the political agendas of celebrities of later generations. Not everyone is familiar with Astaire's films so many years later, but he will continue to hold a unique place in American pop culture, and the image of the top hat and coat tails stand as enduring reminders of the power of song and dance to comfort the viewer and lighten even the darkest of moods.

When people think of Ginger Rogers, images of her dancing with Fred Astaire inevitably come to mind. Given the fame of the films she made with him, it is no surprise that the 10-year period of the Astaire and Rogers musicals has almost entirely obscured the many other films she appeared in during her roughly 30 year career. However, while few would deny that the Fred and Ginger musicals represent the hallmark of her career, analyzing her career in its totality exposes the versatility of her acting ability. First reaching fame in the early 1930s with appearances in Busby Berkeley films, the contrast between her earliest musicals and the later (more famous) ones makes it possible to view her career as a useful rubric through which to chart the evolution of the musical as a genre. Moreover, Rogers may not have had the dancing talent of her famous co-star, but the sheer breadth of her cinematic oeuvre reveals an acting ability that was more diverse than that of Astaire. Few actresses danced well enough to star alongside Fred Astaire, yet Ginger's greatest accomplishment may well have been her ability to shift seamlessly from musical to romantic comedy to (later in her career) the women's melodrama and film noir.

In addition to her acting abilities, Ginger's legacy is also tied to her singular star persona. Acting during a time in which the vast majority of Hollywood was politically affiliated with the far left, Rogers and Astaire presented a conservative alternative to liberal Hollywood. While much of Hollywood consisted of political radicals, Rogers possessed a decidedly rural sensibility that she first acquired during her upbringing in Kansas City and Fort Worth and would later lead to the purchase of her ranch in Oregon. The ability to alternate between the glamour of her films and the rural nature of her off-screen persona stands as her most distinctive feature. Movie stars are typically celebrated for their ability to effortlessly convey the spectacular on-screen and off, but perhaps Ginger's greatest accomplishment was her ability to alternate between the two spheres. She was not as intimidating as most actresses, instead establishing a persona that Americans could relate to and easily identify with to the point of placing themselves in her shoes. Indeed, no matter how glamorous she might appear alongside Fred Astaire, she was still very much a woman with a decidedly down-to-earth demeanor, one who could convince Americans that no matter how dire their economic circumstances, they could find relief through dance and the power of entertainment.

Testimonials to Fred Astaire and His Dancing

"The fact that Fred and I were in no way similar - nor were we the best male dancers around never occurred to the public or the journalists who wrote about us...Fred and I got the cream of the publicity and naturally we were compared. And while I personally was proud of the comparison, because there was no-one to touch Fred when it came to 'popular' dance, we felt that people, especially film critics at the time, should have made an attempt to differentiate between our two styles. Fred and I both got a bit edgy after our names were mentioned in the same breath. I was the Marlon Brando of dancers, and he the Cary Grant. My approach was completely different from his, and we wanted the world to realize this, and not lump us together like peas in a pod. If there was any resentment on our behalf, it certainly wasn't with each other, but with people who talked about two highly individual dancers as if they were one person. For a start, the sort of wardrobe I wore - blue jeans, sweatshirt, sneakers - Fred wouldn't have been caught dead in. Fred always looked immaculate in rehearsals, I was always in an old shirt. Fred's steps were small, neat, graceful and intimate - mine were ballet-oriented and very athletic. The two of us couldn't have been more different, yet the public insisted on thinking of us as rivals...I persuaded him to put on his dancing shoes again, and replace me in Easter Parade after I'd broken my ankle. If we'd been rivals, I certainly wouldn't have encouraged him to make a comeback." – Gene Kelly

"Fred taught me a step because I said I can't let this experience be over without my learning something. He taught me the most wonderful Fred Astaire-like step, with an umbrella. It was a complete throwaway; it was almost invisible. It was in the way he walked. As he moved along, he bounced the umbrella on the floor to the beat and then he grabbed it. It was effortless and invisible. As a matter of fact, a few years later I was photographing Gene Kelly and told him that Fred Astaire had taught me this trick with an umbrella. And Kelly said, 'Oh I'll teach you one,' and he did, and the two tricks with the umbrella in some way define the difference between Fred Astaire and Gene Kelly, and, in my view, demonstrate who is the greater of the two artists. With Gene Kelly, he threw the umbrella way up into the air, and then he moved to catch it, very slowly, grabbing it behind his back. It was a big, grandstand play, about nothing." - Richard Avedon

"The major difference between Astaire and Kelly is a difference, not of talent or technique, but of levels of sophistication. On the face of it, Kelly looks the more sophisticated. Where Kelly has ideas, Astaire has dance steps. Where Kelly has smartly tailored, dramatically apt Comden and Green scripts, Astaire in the Thirties made do with formulas derived from nineteenth-century French Farce. But the Kelly film is no longer a dance film. It's a story film with dances, as distinguished from a dance film with a story. When Fred and Ginger go into their dance, you see it as a distinct formal entity, even if it's been elaborately built up to in the script. In a Kelly film, the plot action and the musical set pieces preserve a smooth community of high spirits, so that the pressure in a dance number will often seem too low, the dance itself plebeian or folksy in order to "match up" with the rest of the picture." - Arlene Croce

"I suspect it is this Camelot view that leads Miss Croce to be rather unfair to Gene Kelly...I should say the difference starts with their bodies. If you compare Kelly to Astaire, accepting Astaire's debonair style as perfection then, of course, Kelly looks bad. But in popular dance forms, in which movement is not rigidly codified, as it is in ballet, perfection is a romantic myth or a figure of speech, nothing more. Kelly isn't a winged dancer; he's a hoofer and more earthbound. But he has warmth and range as an actor...Astaire's grasshopper lightness was his limitation as an actor - confining him to perennial gosh-oh-gee adolescence;; he was always and only a light comedian and could function only in fairytale vehicles." - Pauline Kael

"I can watch Astaire anytime. I don't think he ever made a wrong move. He was a perfectionist. He would work on a few bars for hours until it was just the way he wanted it. Gene was the same way. They both wanted perfection, even though they were completely different personalities." - Cyd Charisse

"There never was a greater perfectionist, there never was, and never will be, a better dancer, and I never knew anybody more kind, more considerate, or more completely a gentleman...I love Fred, John, and I admire and respect him. I guess it's because he's so many things I'd like to be and I'm not." – Bing Crosby

"At its most basic, Mr. Astaire's technique has three elements - tap, ballet and ballroom dancing. The ballet training, by his account, was brief but came at a crucial, early age. He has sometimes been classed as a tap dancer, but he was never the hoofer he has jokingly called himself. Much of the choreographic outline of his dancing with his ladies—be it Miss Rogers or Miss Hayworth—is ballroom. But of course, no ballroom dancer could dance like this." - Dance critic Anna Kisselgoff

"Mr. Astaire is the nearest approach we are ever likely to have to a human Mickey Mouse; he might have been drawn by Mr. Walt Disney, with his quick physical wit, his incredible agility. He belongs to a fantasy world almost as free as Mickey's from the law of Gravity." – Graham Greene, movie critic.

"But when you're in a picture with Astaire, you've got rocks in your head if you do much dancing. He's so quick-footed and so light that it's impossible not to look like a hay-digger compared with him." - Bing Crosby

"I work bigger. Fred's style is intimate. I'm very jealous of that when I see him on the small screen. Fred looks so great on TV. I'd love to put on white tie and tails and look as thin as him and glide as smoothly. But I'm built like a blocking tackle." - Gene Kelly

"Just to see him walk down the street ... to me is worth the price of admission." - Sammy Davis Jr.

Bibliography

Altman, Rick. *The American Film Musical*. Bloomington: Indiana University Press, 1987.

Berry, Sarah. *Screen Style: Fashion and Femininity in 1930s Hollywood*. Minneapolis: University of Minnesota Press, 2000.

Croce, Arlene. New York: Galahad Books, 1972.

Evans, Peter Williams. *Top Hat*. Malden: John Wiley & Sons, 2010.

Faris, Jocelyn. *Ginger Rogers: A Bio-Bibliography*. Westport: Greenwood Press, 1994.

Feuer, Jane. *The Hollywood Musical*. Bloomington: Indiana University Press, 1993.

Gallafent, Edward. *Astaire and Rogers*. New York: Cameron Books, 2000.

Kuhn, Annette. *Dreaming of Fred and Ginger: Cinema and Cultural Memory*. New York: New York University Press, 2002.

Nochimson, Martha. *Screen Couple Chemistry: The Power of 2*. Austin: University of Texas Press, 2002.

Rickard, Sue. "Movies in Disguise: Negotiating Censorship and Patriarchy Through the Dances of Fred Astaire and Ginger Rogers." *Approaches to the American Musical*. Ed. Robert Lawson Peebles. Exeter: University of Exeter Press, 1976. 72-88.

Wood, Robin. *Howard Hawks*. Detroit: Wayne State University Press, 2006.

Printed in Great Britain
by Amazon